CONTENTS

WHAT ARE WILDFIRES?

Wildfires are deadly natural disasters. They can happen anytime, anywhere. What's the difference between a fire and a wildfire? Wildfires are unplanned and uncontrolled. They burn natural areas, killing plants, animals, and people as they go. Wildfires can wipe out entire **ecosystems** such as forests and grasslands. They burn down homes and businesses. They also pollute the air. Pollution from wildfires continues to be harmful long after the fires burn out.

VERIFIED

Wildfires are very scary. But there are ways you can help! Check out **www.ready.gov/kids/disaster-facts/wildfires**. You'll find helpful ideas about how to prevent wildfires. You'll also learn what you can do before, during, and after a wildfire to stay safe.

ROSEN Verified
NATURAL DISASTERS

WILDFIRES

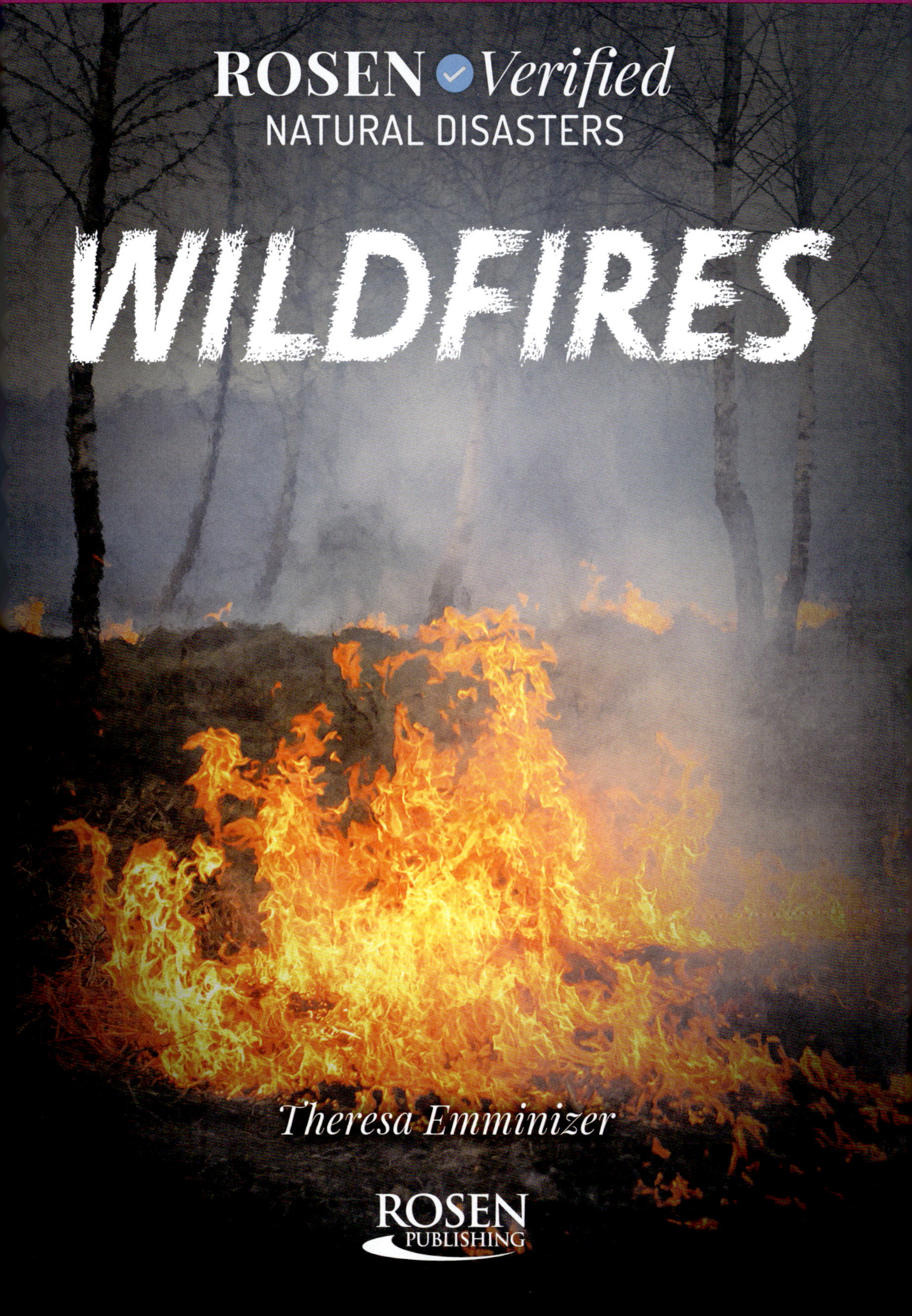

Theresa Emminizer

ROSEN PUBLISHING

Published in 2023 by The Rosen Publishing Group, Inc.
2544 Clinton Street, Buffalo, NY 14224

First Edition

Editor: Theresa Emminizer
Book Design: Michael Flynn

Photo Credits: Cover Vitalii Stock/Shutterstock.com; (series background) PinkPueblo/Shutterstock.com; p. 5 stockpexel/Shutterstock.com; p. 7 orxy/Shutterstock.com; p. 9 emattil/Shutterstock.com; p. 11 nyker/Shutterstock.com; Keith G Webb/Shutterstock.com; p. 15 ZUMA Press, Inc./Alamy Stock Photo; p. 17 J. Emilio Flores/Shutterstock.com; p. 19 (wildfire) Andrew Orlemann/Shutterstock.com; p. 19 (sign) OGdesign/Shutterstock.com; p. 21 https://en.wikipedia.org/wiki/File:The_Peshtigo_Fire_showing_people_seeking_refuge_in_the_Peshtigo_River.jpg; p. 23 David Aughenbaugh/Shutterstock.com; p. 25 REUTERS/Alamy Stock Photo; p. 27 Visual Valor/Shutterstock.com; p. 29 Christie Cooper/Shutterstock.com; p. 30 Anna LoFi/Shutterstock.com; pp. 32-33 Simeonn/Shutterstock.com; p. 35 IM_photo/Shutterstock.com; p. 37 Natural History Archive/Alamy Stock Photo; p. 39 Jessica Gardetto, BLM; p. 41 aappp/Shutterstock.com; p. 43 Logan Bush/Shutterstock.com; p. 45 Pixel-Shot/Shutterstock.com.

Cataloging-in-Publication Data

Names: Emminizer, Theresa
Title: Wildfires, Theresa, Emminizer
Description: New York: Rosen Publishing, [2023] | Series: Rosen Verified : Natural Disasters | Includes index.
Identifiers: ISBN: 9781499473605 (library binding) | 9781499473599 (paperback) | 9781499473612 (ebook)
Subjects: LCSH: Wildfires - Juvenile literature
Classifications: LCC: SD421.23 | DDC 363.379

Manufactured in the United States of America

Some of the images in this book illustrate individuals who are models. The depictions do not imply actual situations or events.

CPSIA Compliance Information: Batch #CWRYA23. For further information contact Rosen Publishing at 1-800-237-9932.

Between January and June 2022, there were 29,966 wildfires within the United States alone. These fires burned about 2,790,609 acres (1,129,319 ha) of land. Across the planet, pollution from wildfires causes more than 33,500 deaths each year. Warming global temperatures are creating hotter, drier conditions that make wildfires more likely. They're also likely to happen more often. What can we do to stop the spread of these deadly disasters? How can we prevent wildfires? How can we be prepared?

Eight of the world's worst wildfire weather years took place within the past 10 years.

HOW DO WILDFIRES START?

Fire needs three things to ignite, or start: heat, fuel, and oxygen (air). Fuel could be wood. It could also be dried vegetation, or plants and leaves.

During certain times of the year, the weather and dryness of plants make wildfires more likely to happen. These are called fire seasons. The U.S. fire season usually lasts from about June until September.

Some wildfires start naturally. Here are the main natural causes:

LIGHTNING

Lightning is probably the biggest natural cause. During a storm, humid, or wet, air rises. This feeds a thunderstorm. Closer to the ground, the air is dry. The dry air **evaporates** the rain before it can reach the ground. This is known as virga. When lightning strikes, or hits, in dry conditions it can start a fire. Fires are usually started by long-lasting, hot bolts of lightning. Once sparked, windy conditions can cause the fire to spread very quickly.

LAVA

Wildfires may also be started by lava. Lava is hot, liquid rock that comes out of a volcano. Although lava itself is not on fire, the heat from lava can ignite dry vegetation. This leads to wildfires.

The 2002 Kupukupu Fire in Hawaii was started by lava from the volcano Kīlauea. It burned more than 3,367 acres (1,363 ha).

1988 YELLOWSTONE FIRES

Yellowstone National Park was the world's first national park. The U.S. government established it in 1872. When it came to wildfires, historically, Yellowstone managers had a "let it burn" policy, or rule. This meant that any fires that started naturally were allowed to burn out on their own. This became a problem during the summer of 1988.

That year, Yellowstone went through the worst drought in its recorded history. For three months, almost no rain fell. Dry storms whipped wind through the park and lightning struck. Fueled by the dry vegetation and strong winds, the park went up in flames.

Lightning strikes started about 42 fires that the summer. Human activities also caused nine fires.

The 1988 fires burned 793,880 acres (321,272 ha). That's about 36 percent of the park's total size. Three hundred large mammals were killed, including 246 elk, 9 bison, 4 mule deer, and 2 moose.

On July 15, park management dropped its "let it burn" policy and began trying to contain the fires. But it wasn't until rain and snow fell in September that the fires finally stopped.

This photo shows a forest fire in the Wyoming part of Yellowstone National Park.

WILDFIRES AND ECOSYSTEMS

Many people blamed Yellowstone management for failing to contain the fires sooner. But there was a good reason they were allowed to burn. The park's fire policy was based on the science of how ecosystems work. In some cases, wildfires benefit ecosystems!

HOW DO WILDFIRES HELP?

- Kill harmful insects
- Burn down diseased, or sick, trees and plants
- Make room for young, healthy trees to grow
- Add **nutrients** to the soil
- Some plants, such as evergreen trees, need heat to release their seeds

Yellowstone **experts** saw that natural fires benefitted the park. A major burn had happened in the area in the 1730s. It seemed that the natural fires of 1988 fit within the ecosystem's burn cycle. Although many large animals were lost in the 1988 fires, there were also ecological benefits.

YELLOWSTONE FIRE MANAGEMENT

Today, Yellowstone's fire policy is still to let nature take its course. Fires sparked by lightning are allowed to burn as long as people and historic landmarks aren't in danger. All fires caused by humans are put out.

Lodgepole pines in Yellowstone need heat to release their seeds.

HUMAN-CAUSED WILDFIRES

Although wildfires are sometimes caused by nature, most often they're started by people. Human activities cause more than 84 percent of wildfires.

TOP 5 LEADING KNOWN CAUSES OF WILDFIRES STARTED BY PEOPLE IN THE UNITED STATES

#1. Burning Debris: People often burn **debris, or unwanted things**, in their backyards. Backyard debris could be leaves, grass, or trash. Burning debris accounts for, or makes up, 29 percent of the fires caused by people.

#2. Arson: Arson is the illegal act of setting fire to property. Even if a person isn't trying to start a fire, they can be charged with arson for ignoring fire rules. About 21 percent of U.S. wildfires are started by arson.

#3. Equipment Use: Using power tools and machines, such as lawnmowers, chainsaws, grills, and even cars improperly can start fires. Misuse of equipment makes up about 11 percent of human-caused wildfires.

#4. Campfires/Fireworks: Campfires must be made and put out safely. Fireworks can be very dangerous if they aren't handled properly. Campfires and fireworks each account for about 5 percent of wildfires started by people.

#5. Smoking: Smoking accounts for 2 percent of human-started wildfires.

Half of all recorded wildfires in the world had unknown causes.

2020 EL DORADO WILDFIRE

Recklessness is acting without thinking about the possible consequences. If a person behaves recklessly with fire or a **pyrotechnic device**, the results can be deadly.

In 2020, a couple in Yucaipa, California, **allegedly** started a wildfire. They were having a "gender-reveal" party to share the sex of their baby. To do this, they set off a colored smoke bomb on September 5, 2020.

The device sparked a fire that spread over two counties. It burned more than 22,000 acres (8,903 ha) and destroyed many homes. Much of the fire was located in San Bernardino National Forest.

On September 17, Charles Morton, a 39-year-old firefighter, died while fighting the fire. Two others were hurt.

A CRIMINAL ACT

The couple who started the fire were charged with **involuntary manslaughter**. They were also charged with three **felony** counts of recklessly causing a fire with great bodily injury, and four felony counts of recklessly causing a fire to inhabited structures (buildings in which people live). Less serious charges included 22 **misdemeanor** counts of recklessly causing fire to property.

This photo was taken September 15, 2020. It shows a helicopter fighting the El Dorado Fire above Angelus Oaks, California.

INTERAGENCY HOTSHOT CREWS

Charles Morton was a firefighter for the U.S. Forest Service for 14 years. The U.S. Forest Service, National Park Service, Bureau of Land Management, and Bureau of Indian Affairs have more than 100 Interagency Hotshot Crews (IHC). IHCs use their special knowledge and skills to attack wildfires. Morton was a **squad** boss for the Big Bear Interagency Hotshot Squad. Hotshots are the special forces of firefighting.

A hotshot is a firefighter who works on the frontlines. They go directly into the hottest, most dangerous parts of the fire. Hotshot crews are made up of highly skilled, highly trained firefighters with lots of experience. Many become Emergency Medical Technicians (EMTs) as part of their training.

A hotshot fights a fire in Santa Clarita, California.

DO YOU HAVE WHAT IT TAKES?

IHC firefighters must pass written and physical tests. Here are some of the physical requirements. Could you be part of an IHC crew?

- 1.5-mile (0.8 km.) run in a time of 10 minutes and 35 seconds or less
- 40 sit-ups in 60 seconds
- 25 push-ups in 60 seconds
- Chin-ups, based on body weight:
    - More than 170 pounds (77 kg) = 4 chin-ups
    - 135–170 pounds (61–77 kg) = 5 chin-ups
    - 110–135 pounds (50–61 kg) = 6 chin-ups

FIRE FACTORS

There are three main elements that affect how a wildfire spreads: fuels, topography, and weather.

FUELS

Fuels are a driving force of wildfire behavior. The amount of moisture, or wetness, in fuel changes how quickly it burns.

TOPOGRAPHY

Topography is the physical features of an area and how they're laid out. Certain features make a fire spread faster. Others create natural firebreaks, stopping its spread. Fires that travel up a slope usually spread faster. That's because hot air rises, heating up vegetation higher on the hill. Topographical features may include:

- **Elevation:** The measurement of an area's height above sea level.
- **Slope:** How steep the land is and which direction a slope is facing.
- **Features:** Waterways such as rivers, lakes, or streams. Land features, such as canyons or cliffs.

WEATHER

Weather includes temperature, humidity, and wind. Wind feeds wildfires by providing oxygen. It also directs where the fire will spread. Strong winds can create firestorms. Firestorms are created when heat from a wildfire causes its own wind system. Firestorms are very destructive and **violent**. The strong winds fuel the blaze and pull things into it.

Fire experts refer to these factors as the "fire behavior triangle."

THE GREAT PESHTIGO FIRE

The Great Peshtigo Fire was the deadliest fire in U.S. history. It began on October 8, 1871, in Peshtigo, Wisconsin. It was over by the next morning. In that short time, between 1,200 and 2,500 people lost their lives. The exact number of dead is unknown. Thousands more became homeless. Over 1,500 were injured. The entire town of Peshtigo was destroyed as were 16 other towns. The fire covered 1.3 million acres (526,000 ha).

People who survived the Peshtigo Fire said it looked and moved like a **tornado**. That's because the weather conditions and fuel in the area combined to create a firestorm. The rushing winds pulled entire houses and buildings into the flames. The fire was so strong that it moved over the waters of Green Bay and the Peshtigo River. Otherwise, they would have been natural firebreaks, or something that stops a fire.

WHAT CAUSED THE PESHTIGO FIRE?

The cause of the Peshtigo Fire is still unknown. Experts think many smaller fires combined to create the larger wildfire. Peshtigo was a lumber town filled with trees and wooden buildings. The summer of 1871 had little rainfall and led to dangerously dry conditions in the town.

This drawing shows townsfolk running to the river to escape the Peshtigo Fire.

CONTAINING WILDFIRES

The U.S. Forest Service oversees the containment of wildland fires. Containment refers to how much of a wildfire's **perimeter** burns freely and how much is controlled. This is talked about in percentages. When a wildfire is 100 percent contained, it's considered over.

WHO FIGHTS WILDFIRES?

Incident Management Teams (IMTs): Professional emergency **response** workers.

Ground Firefighters

- **Handcrews:** 20-person teams who build fire lines to contain fires.
- **Hotshots:** Highly skilled firefighters who attack the hottest, most difficult points of a fire.
- **Engine Crews:** Firefighters who work on engines to carry special equipment to fight wildfires.

Aerial (airborne) firefighters

- **Smokejumpers:** Firefighters who **parachute** from airplanes.
- **Helitack Crews:** Firefighters who **rappel** from helicopters to fight fires.

WHAT DO THEY USE?

- **Fire Retardants:** Water mixed with other ingredients. Used to slow down and cut back a wildfire so that ground fighters can make their way into it.
- **Hand Tools:** Rakes, axes, and blades.
- **Fire Engines:** Trucks used to carry crews, hoses, and tools to the fire.
- **Personal Protective Equipment (PPE):** Fire-resistant clothing, helmets, boots, gloves, and shelters. These protect firefighters from flames.
- **Airplanes and Helicopters:** Aircraft used to drop fire retardants and carry crews and equipment.
- **Modular Airborne Firefighting Systems (MAFFS):** Airtankers used to drop fire retardant.

A helicopter drops fire retardant to contain a California wildfire.

2016 SOBERANES FIRE

The 2016 Soberanes Fire in Monterey, California, took 12 weeks to contain fully. The cost of fighting the fire was $250 million. That made it one of the most costly wildfires in California's history.

The Soberanes Fire started July 22, 2016. It was caused by an illegal campfire that was left unwatched. Within the first week, the fire destroyed 68 structures. It continued to burn across 132,137 acres (53,473 ha). That's about four times as large as San Francisco!

The Soberanes Fire wasn't 100 percent contained until October 13, 2016. It was considered an active fire for 83 days.

TOUGH TERRAIN

What made the Soberanes Fire so hard to contain? The terrain, or land, was the biggest problem. The Soberanes Fire started in Garrapata State Park and burned into parts of the Los Padres National Forest. This land is full of rocky cliffs that are hard for ground firefighters to get to. Firefighters were in danger of being unable to escape if the wind shifted the fire. Aerial firefighters couldn't reach certain areas either.

Firefighters hike to reach the Soberanes Fire in the Carmel Highlands on July 27, 2016.

2018 CAMP FIRE

On November 8, 2018, a fire started on Camp Creek Road in Butte County, California. The fire spread quickly, turning into the sixth-deadliest wildfire in U.S. history.

The 2018 Camp Fire covered 153,336 acres (62,053 ha). It burned 18,804 structures. Many people lost their homes and businesses. Eighty-five people lost their lives. Two people went missing. Seventeen were injured.

The 2018 Camp Fire burned for about 17 days. With the help of a winter rainstorm, firefighters officially contained the fire on November 25, 2018. Though this wildfire burned for more than two weeks, most of the damage happened within the first 4 hours!

Afterward, state fire officials, led a year-long study to find out what had caused it. The fire was started by electrical lines owned by the Pacific Gas & Electric (PG&E) Company.

PG&E FOUND GUILTY

PG&E faced criminal charges for starting the 2018 Camp Fire. The case showed that the company had been warned about its power lines before. PG&E didn't follow state safety rules. Company President Bill Johnson pleaded guilty to 84 counts of involuntary manslaughter. He also pleaded guilty to one felony count of unlawfully starting a fire.

The 2018 Camp Fire burned most of the town of Paradise, California.

CLIMATE CHANGE AND WILDFIRES

Climate change is the long-term change in Earth's climate. Climate is the average weather conditions of a place over a period of time. It's mainly caused by human activities, such as burning fossil fuels (gas, oil, and coal) for power. Burning fossil fuels releases harmful gases called carbon dioxide and methane. These gases trap heat in Earth's atmosphere. This causes Earth's temperature to rise. Warmer, drier conditions increase the chance of wildfires.

HOW HAS CLIMATE CHANGE AFFECTED WILDFIRES?

- The average wildfire season is now three and a half months longer than it was in the past.
- Wildfires now burn double the acreage.

VERIFIED

Climate change isn't just affecting wildfires. It's also increasing the likelihood, or chance, of other kinds of natural disasters. These natural disasters are often more intense, or stronger, than they used to be. Check out this site to learn more about climate change: **climatekids.nasa.gov/kids-guide-to-climate-change/**. You'll learn more about why climate change is happening, why it matters, and what you can do about it.

If Earth's temperatures continue to rise, we can continue to expect wildfires to worsen in the years to come.

2019–2020 AUSTRALIAN BUSHFIRES

The Australian Bushfires began in June 2019. They burned until March 2020. During that time the fires spread across 46 million acres (18.62 million ha). They destroyed more than 5,900 buildings, including 2,779 homes. Thirty-four people lost their lives.

The 2019-2020 Australian Bushfires burned for almost 240 days.

The 2019-2020 Australian Bushfires season was one of the worst wildlife disasters in history. Millions of animals were killed or lost their homes. One-third of the world's koala population was lost.

There were several climate factors that led to the Australian wildfires. The following chart lists a few.

CONTRIBUTING FACTORS

- 107.42°Fahrenheit (41.9°C)
- 2019 was Australia's hottest year on record. It was 1.5°C above the long-term 1961–1990 average.
- Australia had its driest ever year in 2019. Rainfall was 40 percent lower than the 1900–2019 average.

VERIFIED

The World Wildlife Fund was part of the emergency response to the Australian bushfires. You can check out their website—**www.wwf.org.au/what-we-do/bushfires**—to find out more. You can watch a video about the bushfires and read stories. You can learn what steps are being taken to restore the land and wildlife.

DEADLY DAMAGE

Wildfires have lasting health consequences. If people are unable to evacuate, or escape, in time, they may be killed. In addition to burns, people can be harmed by the pollution created by wildfires. Wildfire smoke pollutes the air and water. It remains long after a wildfire burns out.

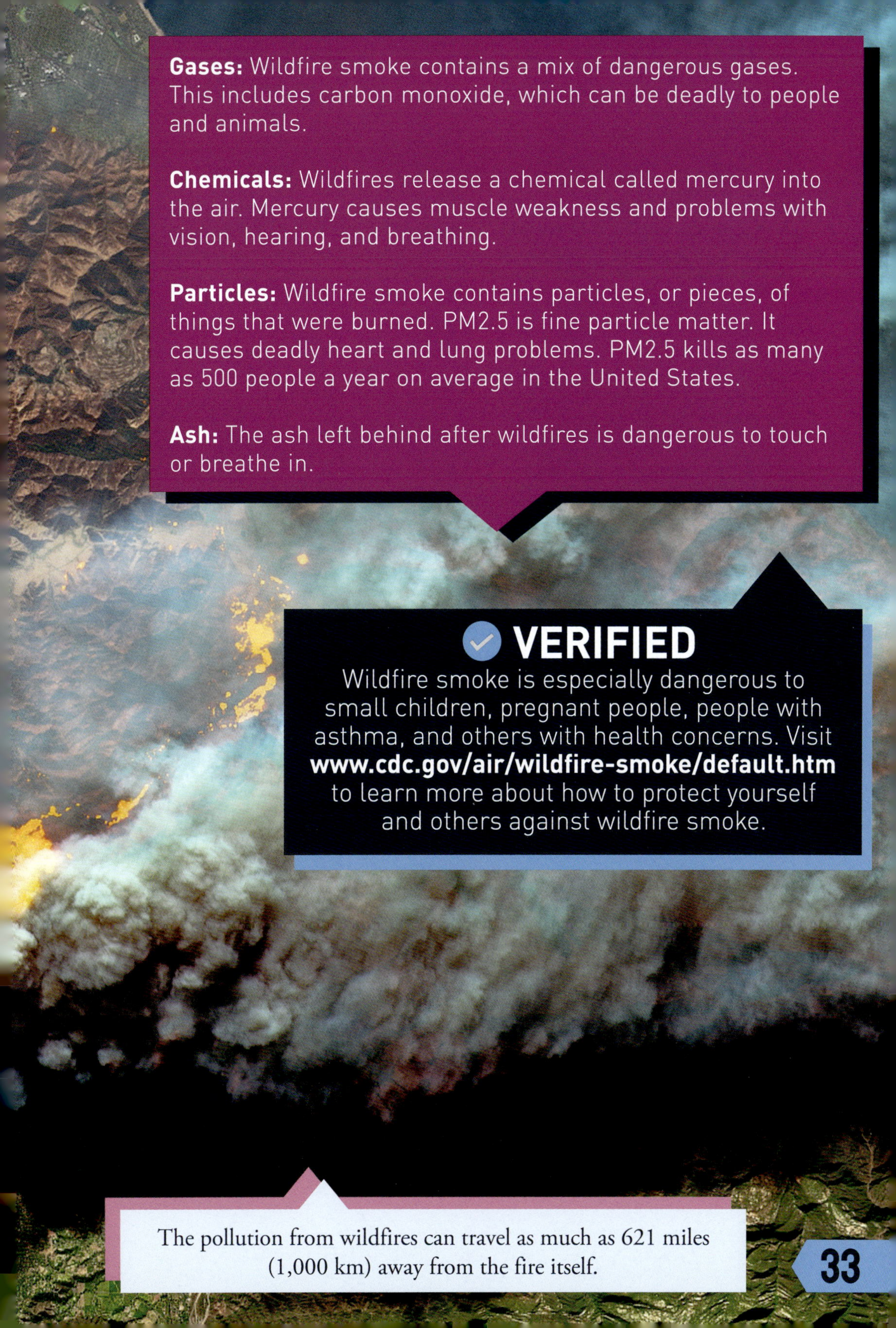

Gases: Wildfire smoke contains a mix of dangerous gases. This includes carbon monoxide, which can be deadly to people and animals.

Chemicals: Wildfires release a chemical called mercury into the air. Mercury causes muscle weakness and problems with vision, hearing, and breathing.

Particles: Wildfire smoke contains particles, or pieces, of things that were burned. PM2.5 is fine particle matter. It causes deadly heart and lung problems. PM2.5 kills as many as 500 people a year on average in the United States.

Ash: The ash left behind after wildfires is dangerous to touch or breathe in.

VERIFIED

Wildfire smoke is especially dangerous to small children, pregnant people, people with asthma, and others with health concerns. Visit **www.cdc.gov/air/wildfire-smoke/default.htm** to learn more about how to protect yourself and others against wildfire smoke.

The pollution from wildfires can travel as much as 621 miles (1,000 km) away from the fire itself.

ECOLOGICAL CONSEQUENCES

Wildfires have lasting ecological consequences. Sometimes ecosystems are damaged beyond repair. What are some of the ways that wildfires affect the environment?

Water Quality: After a fire, the soil is unable to absorb, or take in, water. This creates runoff, or rain that moves over the ground. Runoff carries pollutants from burnt structures into lakes, rivers, and streams.

Loss of Biodiversity: Biodiversity refers to the different kinds of organisms (living things) in an environment. When organisms are killed in a wildfire, biodiversity is lost. Some species may go extinct (die out completely).

Soil Erosion: Roots and vegetation are burned making soil looser and drier. This leads to erosion, or the wearing away of Earth's surface. High temperatures also kill soil's nutrients, making it harder for new plants to grow.

Carbon Emissions: Carbon dioxide, methane, and carbon monoxide are released. These gases are harmful. They also become trapped in the atmosphere, further contributing to global warming. In 2020, California wildfires released the same amount of harmful gases as 24.2 million cars in one year!

VERIFIED
Visit **www.fs.usda.gov/pnw/page/fire-effects-environment** to learn more about how wildfires affect the environment.

This is a giant sequoia tree. In 2020, the Castle Fire in California killed 10 percent of the world's giant sequoia trees.

RESTORATION

The U.S. Forest Service has a special program to repair the damage left by wildfires: BAER. BAER is short for Burned Area Emergency Response. BAER teams find and fix the biggest problems created by wildfires. Sometimes this starts before a wildfire is fully contained.

A BAER team's first goal is to stabilize the area as quickly as possible. They may start by planting seeds, spreading mulch, or putting up walls to stop soil erosion. Controlling erosion is a key part of stopping pollutants from spreading into waterways. Next, they may remove dangerous debris and put up warning signs. They block off recovering areas and remove non-native plants.

BAER teams move in quickly to stop a wildfire's damage from spreading. But it can take many years for an environment to recover. There's often only enough money to work on part of the damaged area for a short time. After the BAER team leaves, there's still work to do.

BAER TEAMS

Who works on a BAER team? Many different specialists, scientists, and engineers work together to restore the areas affected by wildfires.

These workers are rebuilding a trail that was burned in a wildfire at the Grand Canyon in 2000.

FIRE FORECASTING

Fire forecasting is the process of studying weather and fuel conditions to learn about wildfire risk and fire behavior. Fire forecasting saves lives. Understanding how a wildfire may behave means agencies can prepare people to evacuate dangerous areas. Firefighters can come up with a containment plan and be on location ahead of time, ready to fight the fire before it spreads.

FIRE FORECASTING TOOLS

- **Fire Danger Maps:** Used to rate fire danger and show how fires may spread.
- **Haines Index:** A wildfire index that measures how wildfires may grow.
- **Satellites: Infrared** sensors are used to spot wildfires from afar.
- **Weather Data:** Measures wind, rain, humidity, and temperature and how they may affect a fire.

VERIFIED

The Predictive Services program gathers fire forecast data. Predictive Services then shares this with organizations to help them decide how to manage wildfires. Predictive Services teams work at the National Interagency Coordination Center and Geographic Area Coordination Centers across the United States. You can visit **www.predictiveservices.nifc.gov/outlooks/outlooks.htm** to check out current and upcoming fire outlooks.

The National Interagency Fire Center is in Boise, Idaho. President Joe Biden is pictured here, visiting the center in 2021.

FUTURE FIRE TECHNOLOGY

NASA has made new satellite **technology** to help stop wildfires from space. The system is called FireSat. It has more than 200 **thermal** infrared imaging sensors to spot wildfires.

FireStat's sensors can pick up images of wildfires about 30 to 50 feet (9 to 15 m) wide. They do so within 15 minutes of when the fire starts. Within 3 minutes, FireSat sends a message to emergency responders near the fire.

FireSat is not in use today. Although there are satellites that help spot wildfires, they only do so once in a while. The data takes a long time to reach responders on the ground. This means the fire has likely grown by the time firefighters can get to it.

The goal of FireSat is to be on the lookout 24 hours a day, worldwide. It's made to spot fires faster and alert emergency responders quicker.

ROBERT STAEHLE

Robert Staehle is the lead designer of FireSat at NASA's Jet Propulsion Laboratory. Staehle and his team first presented the concept, or idea, of FireSat in 2011. Since then, they've worked on testing it and making it better.

As climate change increases wildfires worldwide, NASA may be called upon to put FireSat to use.

PRACTICE FIRE SAFETY

Wildfires are deadly natural disasters. They have the power to destroy ecosystems, take lives, and pollute the environment. But you have the power to prevent them. Most wildfires are caused by human activities. You can help protect our planet just by practicing fire safety!

FIRE SAFETY TIPS

- Never play with matches or lighters.
- Make sure your home has smoke alarms on every floor, especially in bedrooms.
- Don't have a fire during fire season or during dry or windy conditions.
- Never leave a fire unwatched.
- Pour water on a campfire and stir the ashes cold to put it out completely.
- Never burn cans or glass bottles. They may explode.
- Call 911 if you see a fire or if your fire grows out of control.
- Never throw cigarettes or matches out a car window.
- Keep a shovel, water, and fire retardant (such as a fire extinguisher) nearby when burning a campfire or backyard fire.
- Clear leaves, grass cuttings, and dead tree branches from your yard.

VERIFIED

Visit **smokeybear.com/en/smokey-for-kids** to learn more about fire safety. Smokey has five rules for preventing forest fires. Your actions can make a difference.

You can help prevent wildfires!

WHAT CAN YOU DO?

Forests release oxygen, giving us the air we need to breathe. They also help lower Earth's temperature. They're home to countless plant and animal species. Every year, an average of 1.2 million acres (486,000 ha) of woodland are burned in the United States. Climate change is causing that number to increase.

As the likelihood of wildfires continues to increase, it's important to be prepared. Follow this simple list of dos and don'ts to stay safe if you ever find yourself in a wildfire!

DON'T	DO
Wait at home.	If told to evacuate, do so as quickly as you can.
Try to outrun a fire.	Find a body of water, such as a pond or stream, and crouch close to it.
Hide in a tree.	If you can't find water, find a cleared area with no plants in it and lie on the ground. Cover yourself in wet soil if you can.
Hold your breath.	Breathe in air closest to the ground.

Talk to your family about making a fire safety plan in your home.

Most importantly, if you cause a fire that grows out of control DON'T run away or pretend it didn't happen. DO call 911 as quickly as possible.

GLOSSARY

allegedly: Something that is claimed to have taken place.

ecosystem: A natural community of living and nonliving things.

evaporate: To change from a liquid into a gas, or vapor.

expert: Someone who has a special skill or knowledge.

felony: A serious crime.

infrared: Electromagnetic radiation with wavelengths longer than visible light.

involuntary manslaughter: The crime of killing another person unintentionally, or accidentally.

misdemeanor: A crime less serious than a felony.

nutrient: Something taken in by a plant or animal that helps it grow and stay healthy.

parachute: To fall slowly back to the ground using something shaped like an umbrella.

perimeter: The outer limits of an area.

pyrotechnic device: An explosive, such as a firework.

rappel: To descend, or go down, by sliding down a rope.

response: A reaction or reply.

satellite: A spacecraft placed in orbit around Earth, a moon, or a planet to collect information or for communication.

squad: A small group taking part in a common effort.

technology: The way people do something and the tools they use.

thermal: Having to do with heat.

tornado: A violent, spinning column, or cone, of air.

violent: Having to do with the use of force to cause harm.

INDEX